THIS BOOK BELONGS TO:

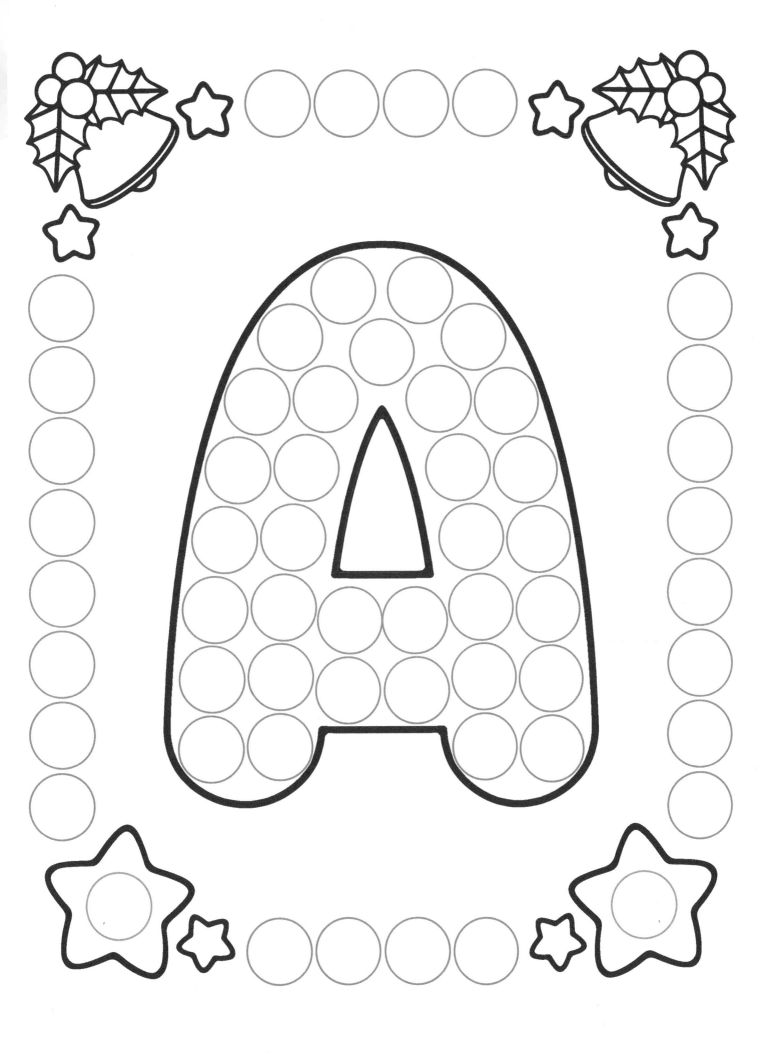

CANDY CANE

ELF

GIFT

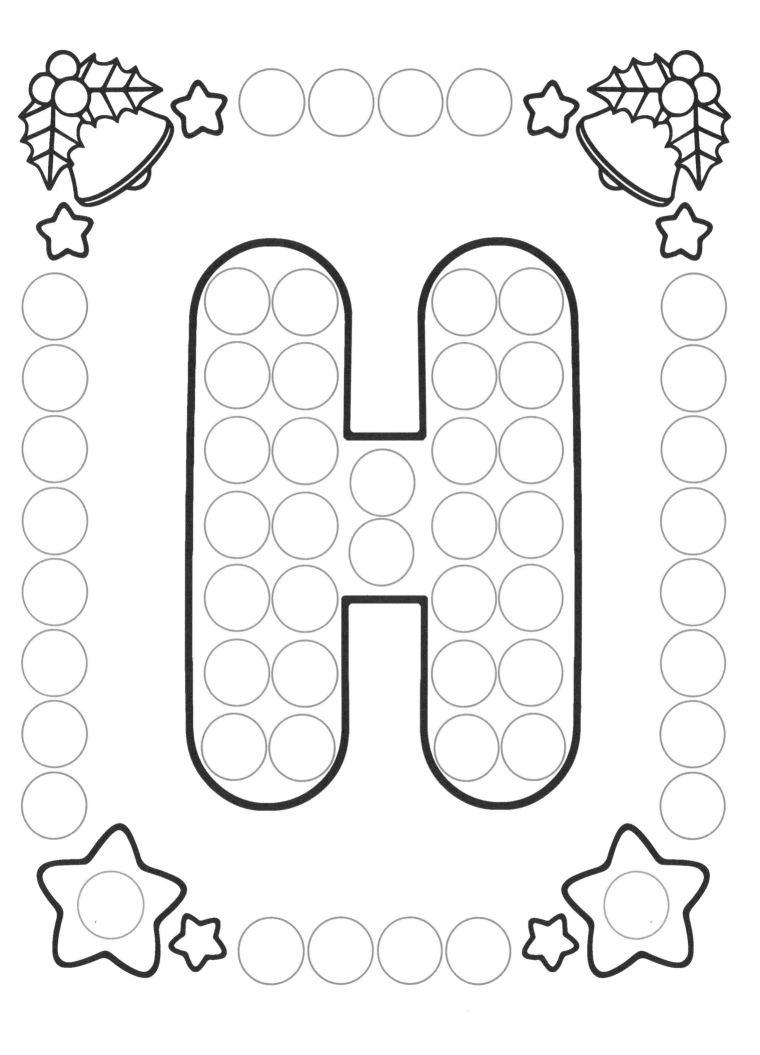

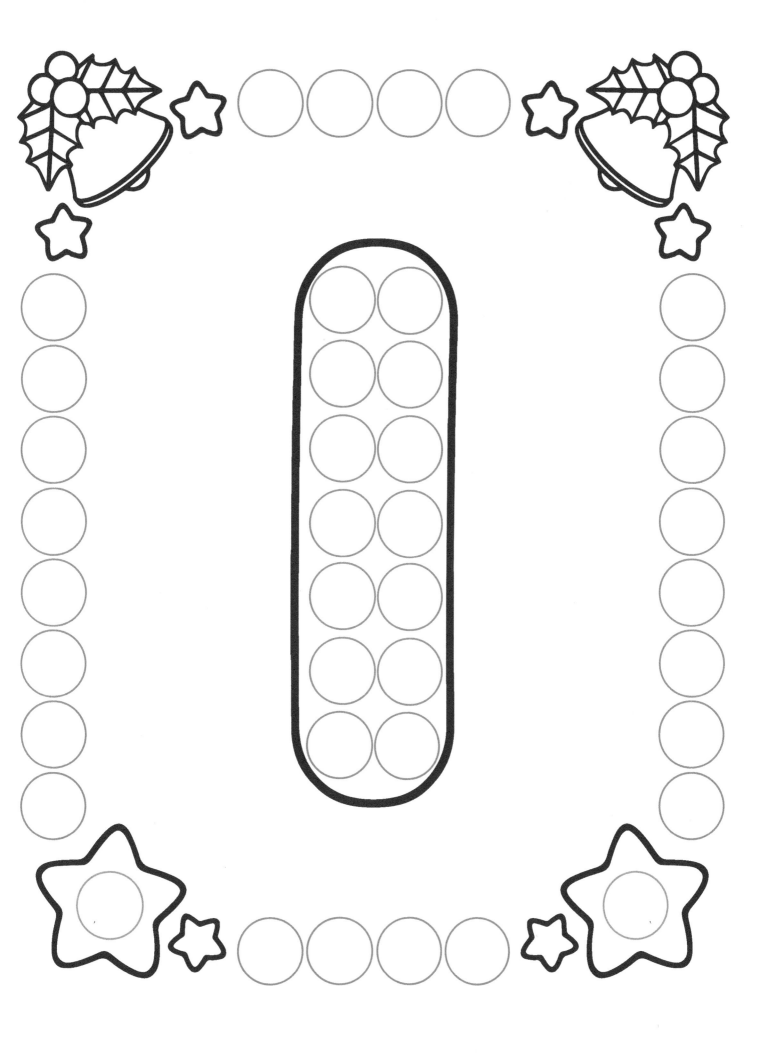

IVY

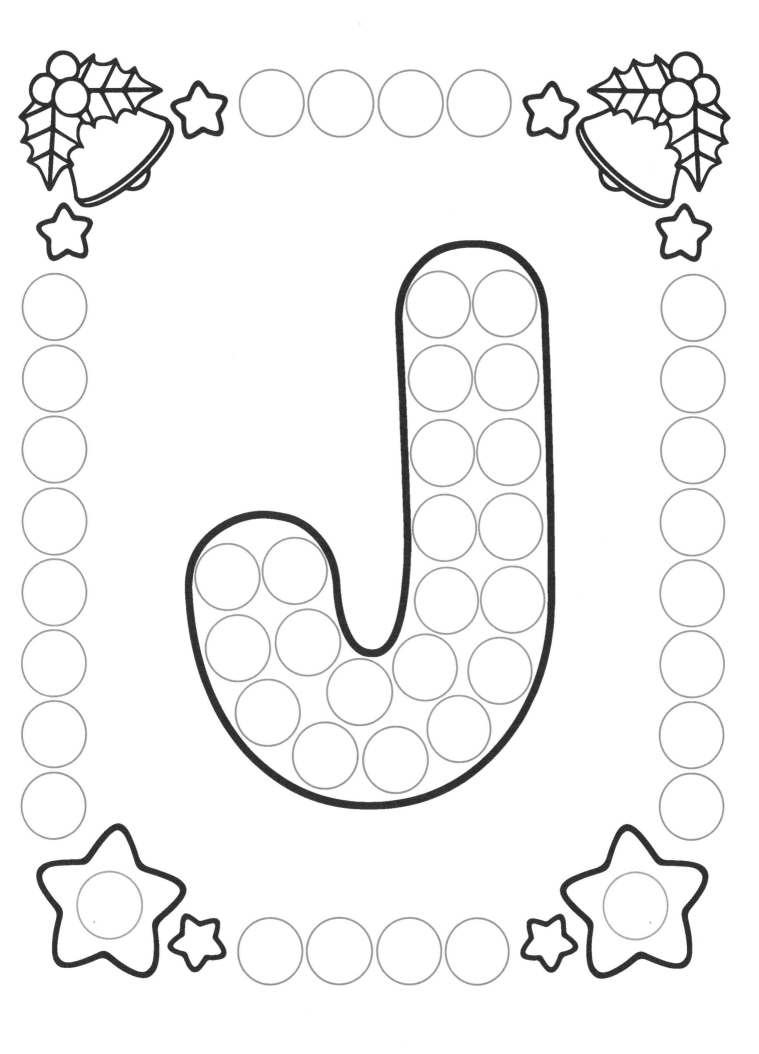

JESUS CHRIST

LETTER

Dear Santa

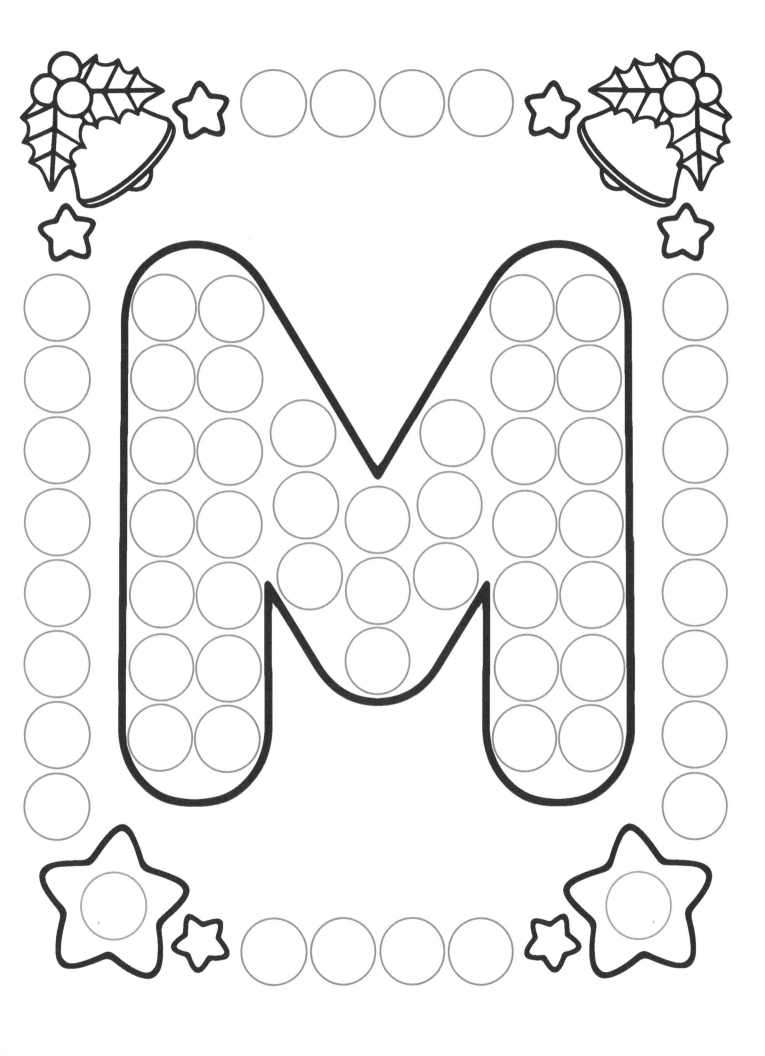

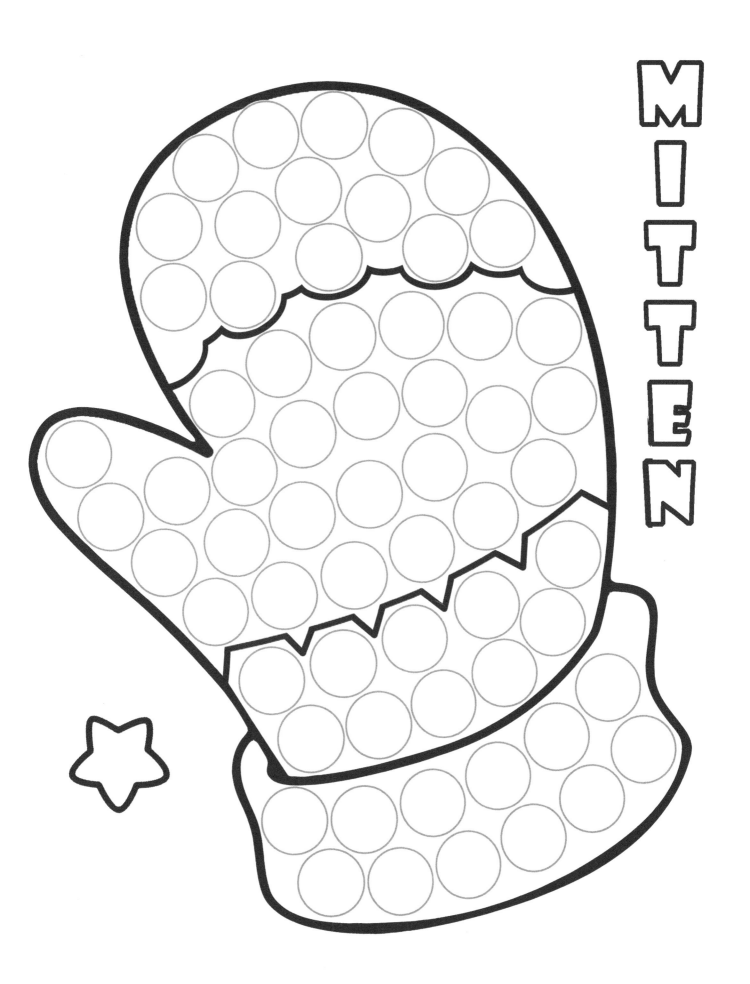

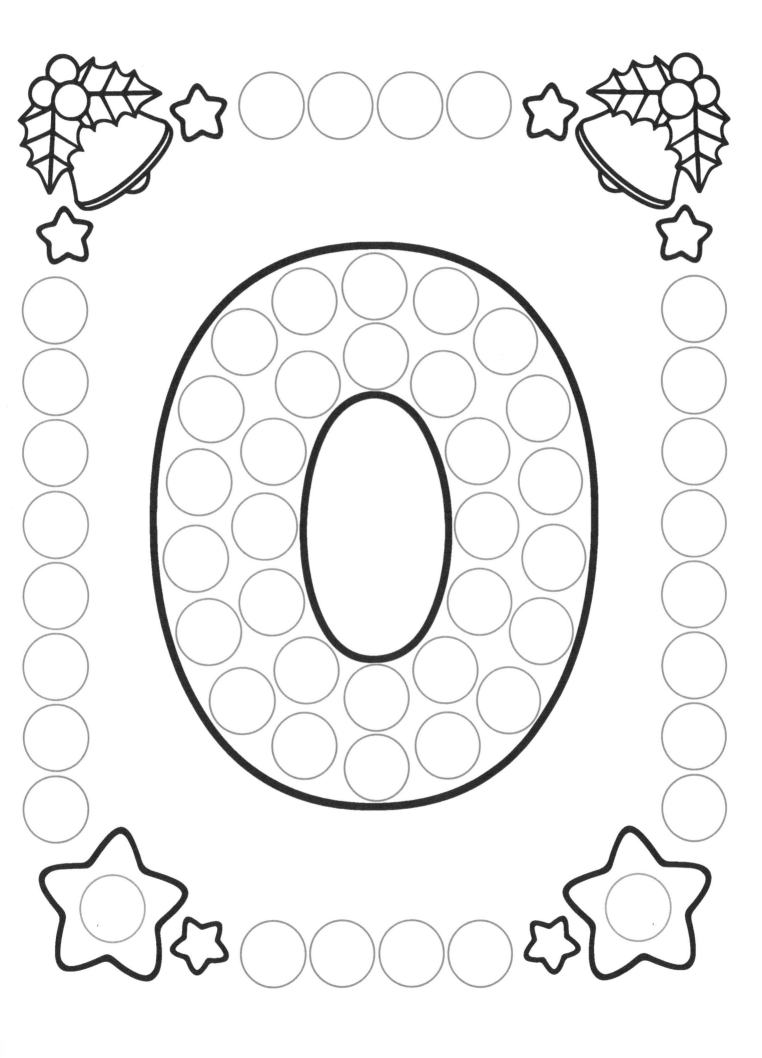

ORNAMENTS

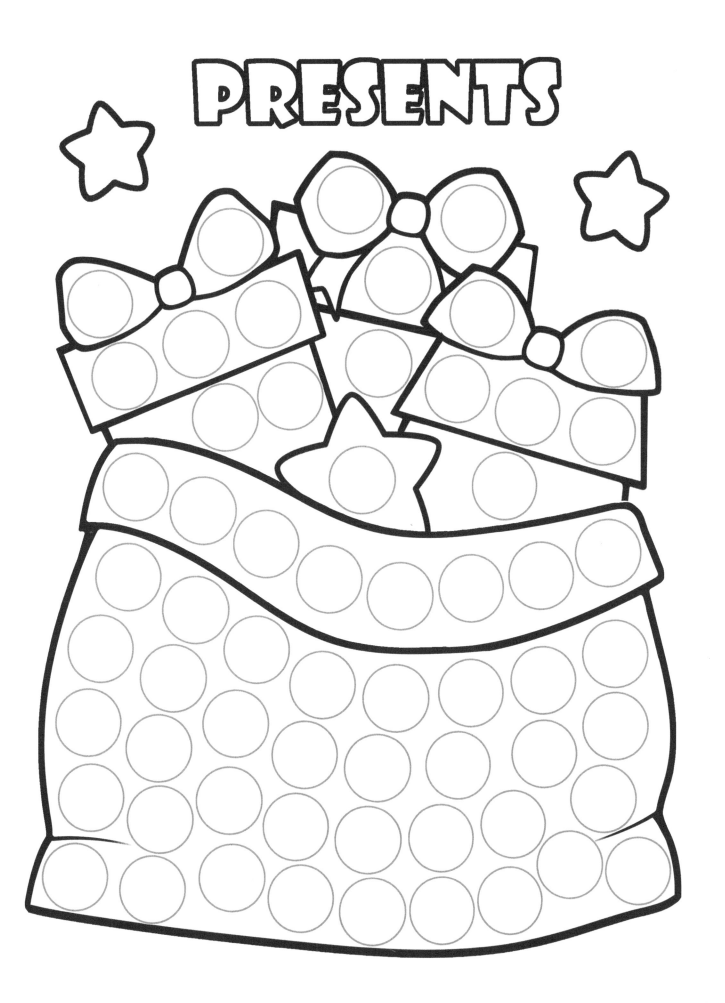

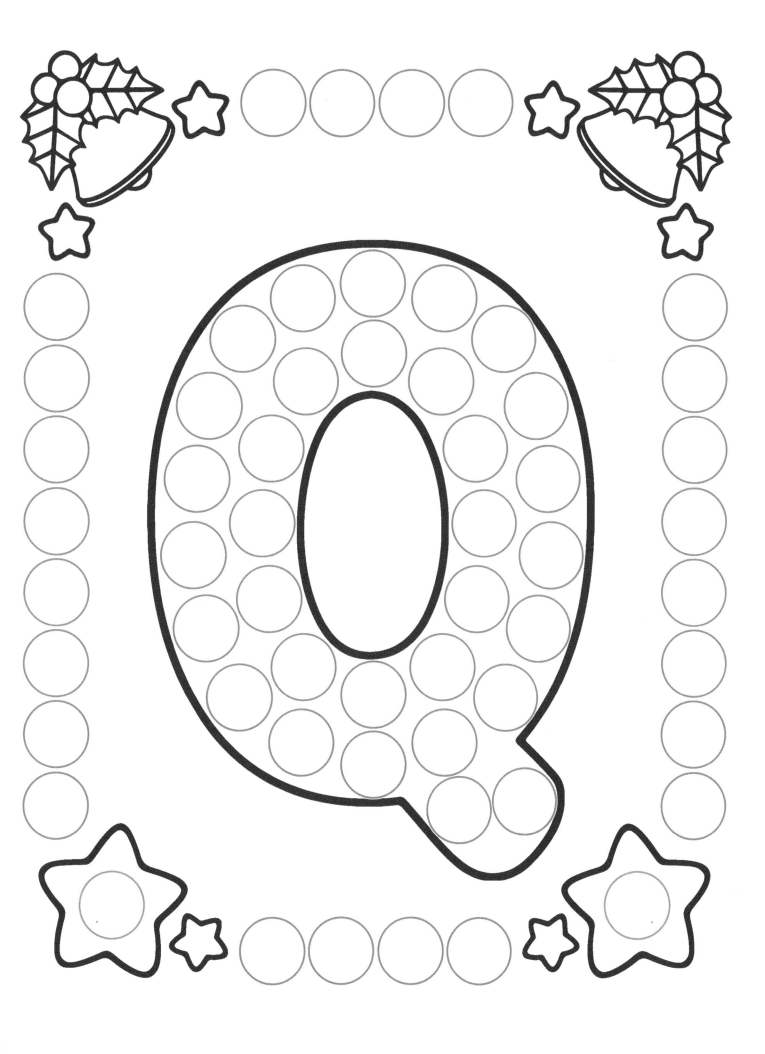

SNOWMAN

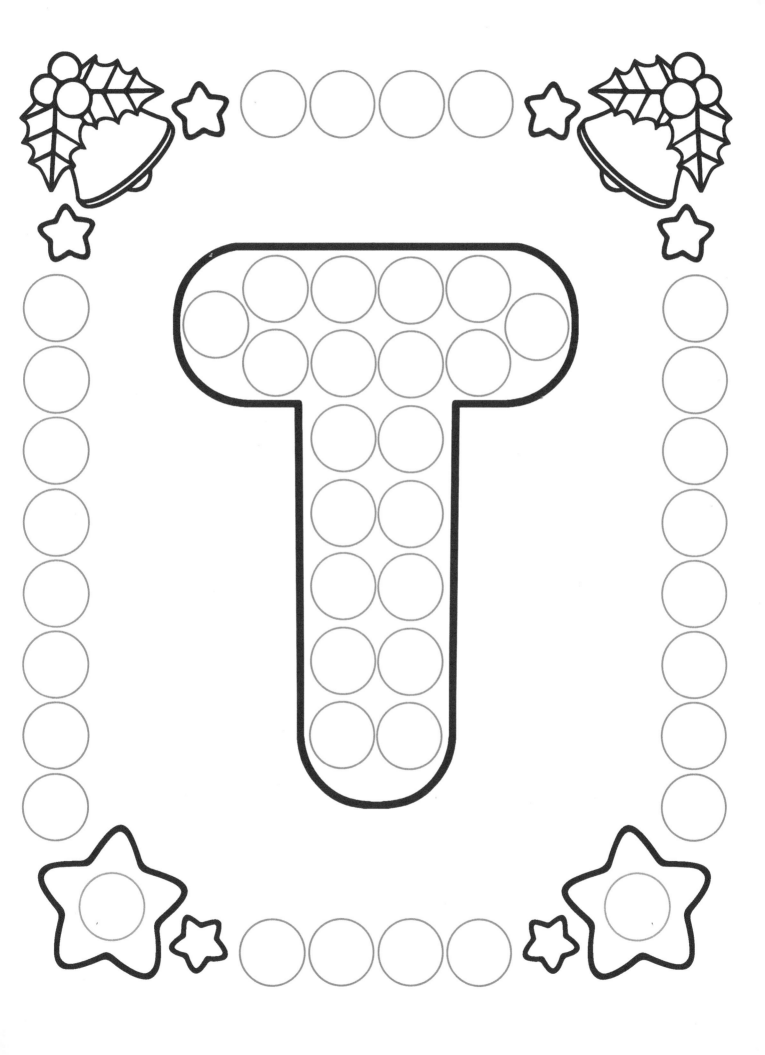

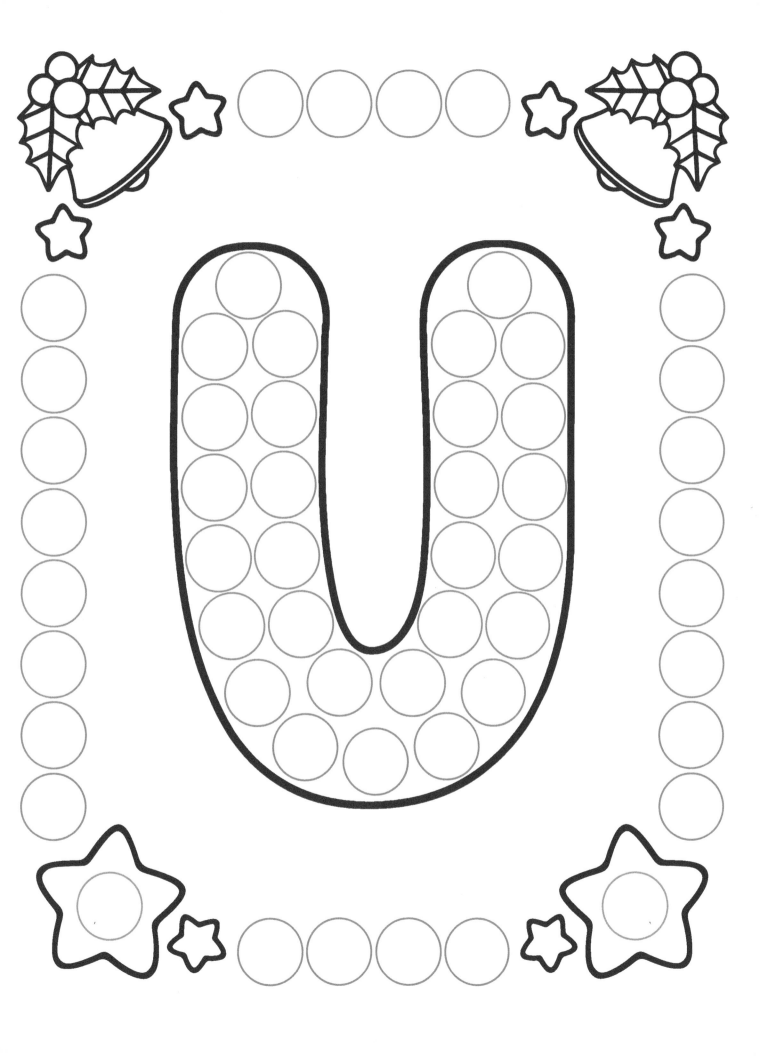

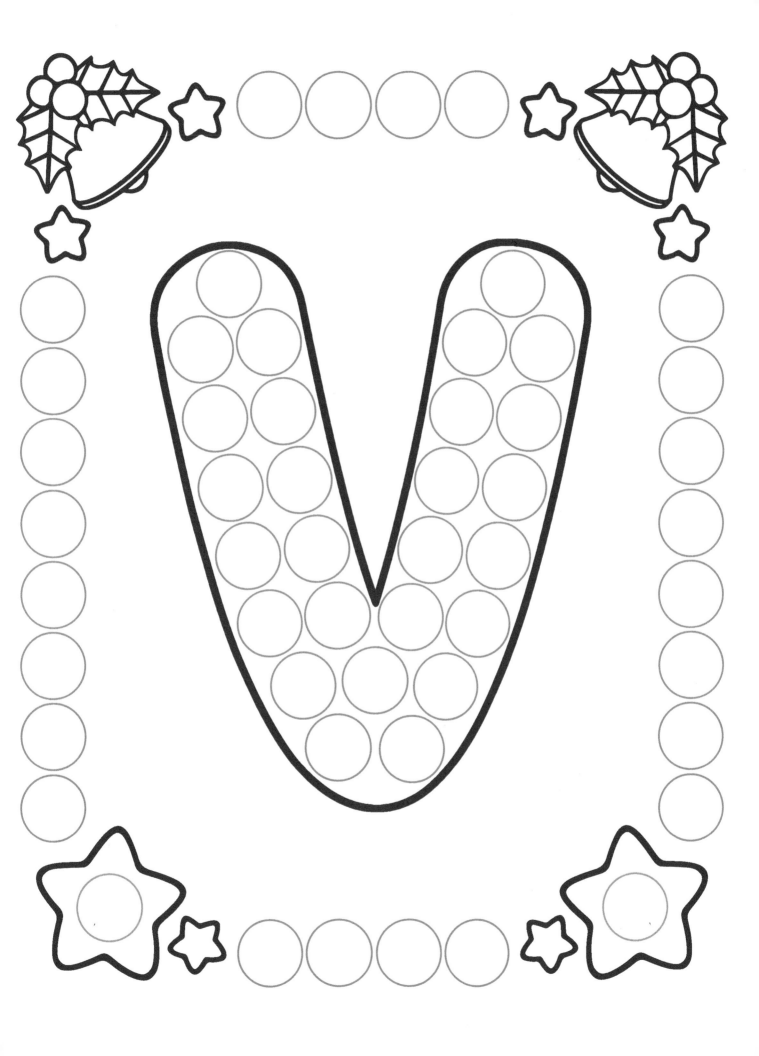

VANILLA

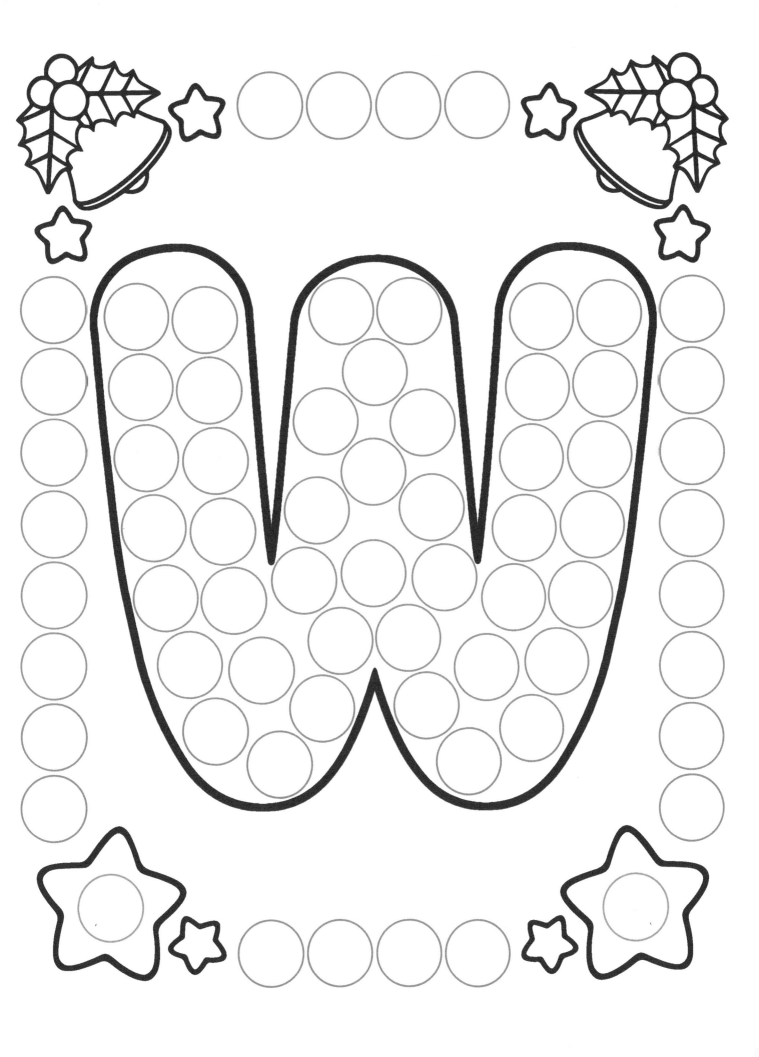

WREATH

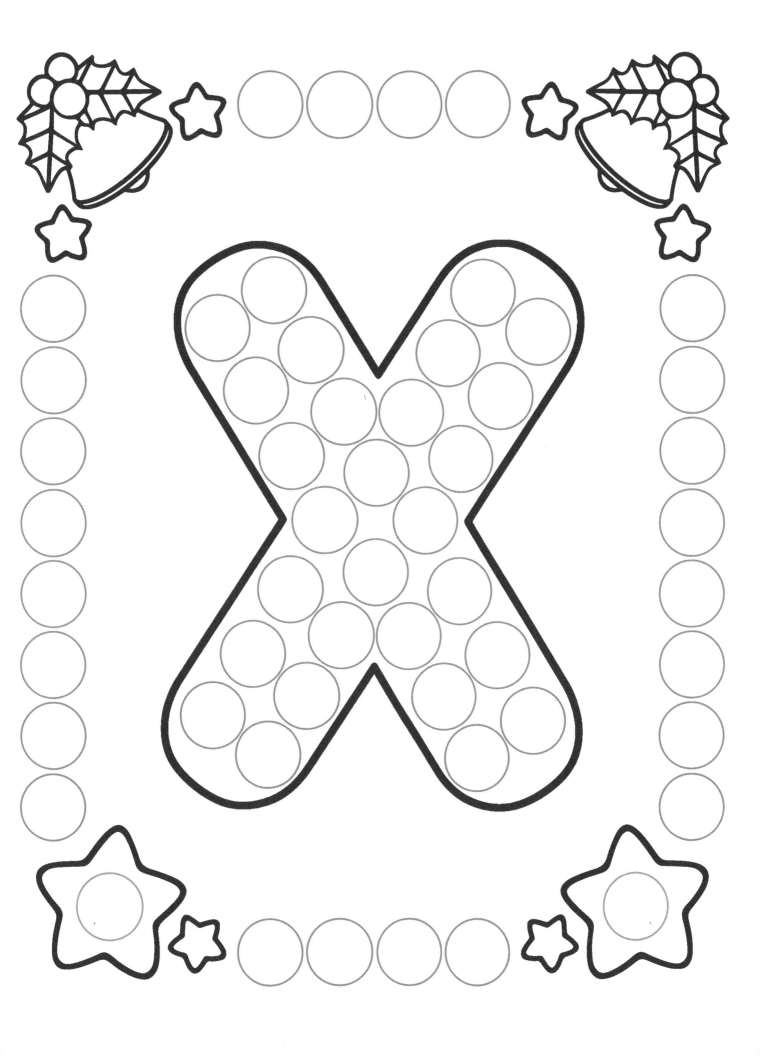

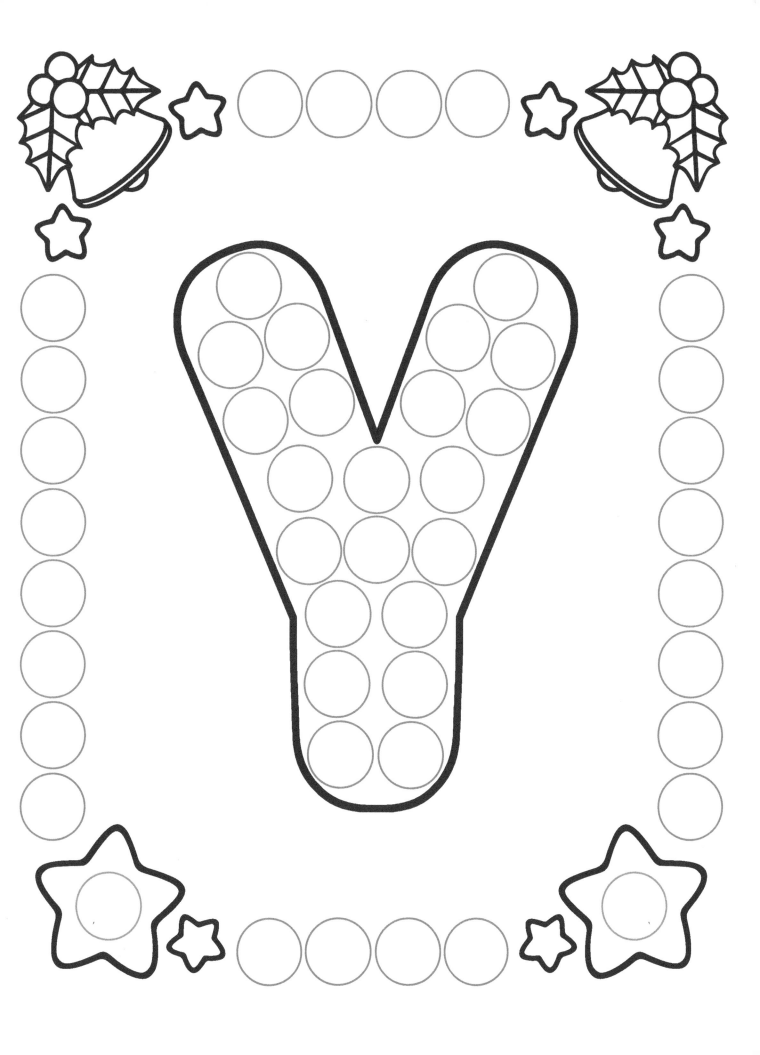

ZESTFUL CHRISTMAS PUDDING

We would love your feedback
on our book.
Please leave a rating if you can!
Thank you!

Made in United States
Cleveland, OH
19 December 2024

12350564R00059